BLIND FAITH AND THE 21ST CENTURY

ROHIT V KOTHAVALE

Contents

Acknowledgements

Time: 5:30 AM

Place: A chair, right next to my bedroom's window.

Sitting on the chair next to my bedroom's window, I looked at a sparrow's nest. I looked closer and found harmony in the sparrow's chirping. The bright twilight provided clarity by its white coloured clear light. After staying awake for the entire night, I started thinking about the darkness my life was taking me to. My future did not have any of the attributes of success that were defined by the society. In a world where even graduation wasn't enough, me an undergrad, found myself to be equivalent to an Angootha chap in Hindi and an illiterate in English. The second attribute talked about a respectable profession (job, business or self-employment); I had none. Tired of finding the right profession, I had given it all up and convinced myself that business was the only option, as it would provide enough green to buy the lavish life that I always dreamt of. I had convinced myself that no job was meant for me. I even convinced myself that I was meant to be employer, not an employee. The very idea of starting a business of my own intrigued me, as it seemed to be something that I could design and control.

After spending 2 years, pursuing an idea that didn't even exist, I found myself sitting right where I was when I started the pursuit. It was ironic that after running behind a mirage for a long time, I could find myself at the same place, staring at the same nest. The only difference was that I failed to find harmony in the sparrow's chirping; the same chirping sounded like millions of needles piercing my heart. It reminded me of the silence in my life.

The man who had found harmony in the chirping was a man who did not possess any of the attributes that defined a so called successful man. The other person was wounded as he did not have any either. However, the second person was wearing the mask of a rich and a successful man. He was living a lavish life that he had dreamt of. He rented an apartment in a high standard building. He wore clothes of a rich man and drove a fancy car. But all of that wasn't bought by giving up the fruits of his efforts; it all came by selling his father's house. All of it was his, but he failed to own it, as it wasn't bought in exchange of the green that he had earned.

I felt an itchiness of discomfort in the very clothes that I called my own. I was living a lavish life that I always dreamt of. But, I had missed an important step that I failed to find in the real world; it was a profession, a source of income. I had spent most of the fortunes that I had gained by selling the house that my father had left behind. Even after calculating a numerous times, I found that the only way to continue living a lavish life was to get a job. Getting selected for a job wasn't difficult, but it was painful to become an employee of an LOB (Line of Business) that I did not design and could not control. Life has its own way of surprising its audience. The chirping sound was once a harmony and sometime later as a bunch of needles piercing the heart of the same person who once found harmony in it.

The dissonance that I found in the music of life led to a pursuit to discover harmony in the music of life. This pursuit led to search for the reason behind the chaos that had filled my mind. It led to an all new way of looking at my life. This book is a medium to express and share my new found perception of looking at life.

Awahan

Saare kahi jari eka aunshat samawale
    Mag ka bare kaik prashna mazhya samor ubhe rahile...
    Aunsha che poorna swaroop jewha samor ubhe rahile
    Tewha sarya prashnan chi uttare deoon tyani aaple kaarya nibhawale.......

Introduction

Blind Faith and the 21ˢᵗ Century

-The dissonance of 'Truth'

The act of dissonance lies in shifting of the curtains location. 'Education' acts as curtain, that was once a blindfold

What is blind faith? Blind faith is defined as belief without true understanding, perception, or discrimination. Blind faith is something that needs to be followed without questioning. It originated with the sole purpose of achieving peace and harmony in a society full of chaos. It was practically impossible to explain the importance or the significance of rules. Rules are meant to be broken. So the sole purpose of blind faith must have been lack of opportunity to break the rules. Humans are reluctant to break rules if the consequence of breaking rules leads to a horrible punishment, a punishment that would be given by the almighty himself. Science wasn't as developed as it is today. Even the level of literacy was very low. With casteism, education was only available to the higher castes. So it must have been impossible to explain the purpose or the importance of rules. Today, casteism does not come in the way of literacy. Everyone gets an opportunity to be educated.

What is the connection between literacy and blind faith? Education gives us the ability to question almost everything in this world. It also makes us capable enough to find the answers by asking our teachers, referring book and the latest trend is to Google it. So we think that blind faith does not apply in today's world. This book is not about following blind faith; it's about the delusion that keeps blind faith alive. Each one of us thinks that we are literate. We have the ability to understand the purpose of our beliefs/faith and that they aren't blind. This book might make you rethink on this and make you feel the need for better understanding of the blind faith and that it still exist in the 21st century. It might provoke its readers to address themselves as puppets of the wise.

In the 21st century, humans or the so called common men are nothing but puppets, bound by the strings of their needs, created and defined by the society. The oblivion of life holds the other end of the strings together in the marionette that is held and controlled by the palm of the wise.

CHAPTER ONE

Black cat crossing one's path...

Black cat crossing one's path...

The consequence of a black cat crossing one's path is another blind faith (One of my favourites.) If a black cat crosses your way, what are you supposed to believe? Is it bad luck or good luck? Does it mean that you should go back home and postpone your journey as it isn't right time? The beliefs about this are different in different parts of the world. Some think it is a good omen or good luck, and some think of it to be a bad omen or bad luck.

Before moving ahead, it is important to know why a black cat? Is it because of its colour? Black colour is a colour of bad omen, evil or negativity. What I believe is that it's not the colour that's important. They get the colour because of high melanin colour pigment. This also affects the colour of their eyes, making them yellow. All this makes them scary. Further, black cats are rare. Cats with colours other than black are very easy to find. You can see one walking in your surroundings pretty often. Let's perform an exercise. Try to count the number of times you seen a black cat. I am sure it won't be more than 5, unless you or someone you know has a black cat as a pet. Also the black colour gives it a natural camouflage at night or at a dark place.

Now that one thing is clear that black cats are a rare sight, let us look at what different cultures have to say about sighting a black cat. Black cats are considered lucky in Asia and in the U.K. If you are in Yorkshire, you would consider yourself lucky to pet a black cat. A black cat walking towards you is a good omen, but one walking away from you is a bad omen. Black cats are also considered to be pets of witches as they are possessed by a spirit that helps them in their so called black magic. Now doesn't that contradict the earlier belief? If a black cat is walking towards you, shouldn't that make you a victim of a witch's black magic? How can that be a good omen? Also, you should be felling lucky if it is walking away from you as that might imply that you are not the victim, the person standing on the other side should be worried. Dreaming of a black cat may mean a lot of things. Some find it to be lucky and some might take it as an intuition from their psychic abilities. Now let's look at what the Indian culture has to say to this. In India, it is believed that if a black cat crosses one's path, then he/she is supposed to walk ten steps backwards. Now this is the one that has a logical explanation. Unlike other animals like dogs, cattle, etc., cats have a very flexible body, which also makes them light in weight. So there are a different ways in which they commute. While following a prey, they crawl. They also make use of their flexibility to climb trees or jump over objects like tables, chairs, etc. In short, they normally do not run in a straight line. They run in a straight line only if they are scared. They get scared if they are running away from trouble like fire, or may be someone who is not a cat person has made it run away. So if a cat crosses one's way, then it should not mean anything to that person. The cat is in a hurry. It does not have enough time to spot the right person and then run. It is least bothered. It doesn't even look at the people around it. Then what is the logical explanation behind this? Walking back ten steps gives you enough time to find the reason why the cat is running. It is easier to take a broader look at the situation if you go away from it, as it works the same way like zooming out while taking a photograph. More things fit in a single frame. This gives us an opportunity to analyse the situation and save ourselves from a dangerous situation like fire or a natural calamity.

Now you know what to think/believe next time you find a black cat crossing your path.

Black cat is a metaphor. There are a lot of black cats walking around us. We fail to notice them; because that's the way they are meant to be. These black cats are created and used by the Wise. They are used to manipulate the market, so that it can be controlled or restricted. They can be seen in the form of news, rumours or the latest trend- 'Individual scientific research'.

Scientific research can be easily manipulated. It is a type of survey. It is impossible to test a product on all the consumers. The number of consumers is too high. So a bunch of consumers are chosen and a survey is conducted. A conclusion is then drawn on the based on their response. This is then used to justify the advantages of the product. However, this conclusion has a lot of limitations. It can be easily fabricated by choosing the right participants for the survey. This survey is then used to market the product. The viewers of the advertisements only notice the success of the survey. They fail to notice a small script at the bottom.

It specifies that the scientific research was independent. It may or may not be approved by a recognised organisation. So it may or may not be reliable. Believing in these surveys proves to be an example of blind faith.

Brand endorsement is another example of black cat. Celebrities endorse brands and make advertisements for the same. They claim the product to be great. Some claim to have used it and some even claims it to be the reason for their success. The celebrity's fans watch such advertisements and develop a blind faith in the brands quality. They trust the celebrities blindly, without checking the quality of the product. All such product may or may not be good. Some products like shampoo, beauty cream, etc. need to be chosen on the basis of the consumer's hair type or skin type, respectively. They may or may not be suitable for all the consumers. The consumers choose the product on the basis of the celebrity who has endorsed it. So, even if the product may be good, it may or may not serve its purpose. So, choosing products on the basis of the celebrity who has endorsed it may or may not be fruitful. The product gets sold in high numbers and the celebrities get paid for endorsing it.

In short, the entire population of billions is controlled by cats like these. They act like traffic signals. So instead of looking at the black cats and blindly changing one's path, one should walk ten steps backwards, take a broader look and then choose the right path.

CHAPTER TWO

Non-vegetarians aren't cruel...

Non-vegetarians aren't cruel...

Why do people think that non-vegetarians are cruel? They are the same as vegetarians. Let's first look at the reason why people think they are cruel.

Killer instinct: They kill animals (living beings) to fulfil one of every human being's basic needs – food. In other words, they put an end to the lives of several living beings.

Now, let's look at what vegetarians do. Even they take away the lives of several living beings. Surprised...Let us look how.

What is the most important ingredient of most of the vegetarian dishes? It's some kind of grain, like rice, corn, or the latest trend multigrain bread. Let's look at how grains are grown. A farmer grows the grains. He transforms seedlings into grains by planting them at his farm.

What happens to those plants after the grains are harvested? They are cut down. Several lives are brought to an end with the sole purpose of fulfilling human beings' most important need – food.

Now, allow me to elaborate on this. Aren't plants living beings? Aren't they killed after harvesting? In other words, they put an end to the lives of several living beings.

Please scroll up to find the same closing statement of the 2nd paragraph that talks about killer instinct found in non-vegetarians.

Even the process is quite similar. Both farmer and butcher breed living beings, take good care of them and then take their lives, so that they can be sold in the market. These consumable items then become human beings' meals. Moreover, if we look at the body count, it is higher in the case of vegetarians. Several plants are cut down to prepare one portion of meal. Whereas even one of the smallest prays of the non-vegetarians, chicken can feed two or more.

I am not trying to say that vegetarians are crueller than non-vegetarians. I am just trying to say that both of them fulfil one of their basic needs by proving the most important rule of nature – Survival of the fittest. There is no difference. The only difference is that the animals have the ability to scream, try to save their life, but the plants are unable to do so. That's the reason why watching an animal being killed is not a pleasant sight. This does not make non-vegetarians crueller than vegetarians.

So, now it's up to the readers to decide if I am right or wrong when I say that: Non-vegetarians aren't cruel...

The purpose of writing this article is to eliminate one point of discrimination, as there are more than enough points to discriminate. So instead of discriminating as the cruel and kind, human beings should be classified same as animals: herbivorous and carnivores.

It is very important to find out why different cultures treat non-vegetarians in completely opposite ways. Some culture like Brahmins consider it cruel to kill animals to fulfil one's hunger, while others like Christians, Muslims consider meat to be their staple food. It is nothing but adaptation that causes the difference in opinion. Christians originate from snow covered regions. So, it is easy for them to digest meat as their climatic conditions are in favour. It also gave them body heat, which helped them cope up with the harsh climatic conditions. Muslims originated from deserts, where farming was impossible. Even planting trees was a challenge as only a few species of vegetation could survive. So, eating animals was a more convenient option to them. Hindus originated from regions with a temperate climate. So, digesting high quantities of fat became a challenge. It must have been impossible to explain this to the masses due to the lack of education. This left them with only one choice, blind faith (belief without true understanding, perception, or discrimination). Fear of God lead to an easy means to spread the message and also imparted an unconditional discipline. With such kind of discipline, the followers weren't left with any other option. They had to be vegetarian or non-vegetarian without choice or argument.

Education makes us capable enough to decide what is right or wrong. It helps to find out what might suite the climatic conditions of one's habitat. So instead of following religion blindly, each one of us should try to device their own staple food as people from all the religions have migrated to different parts of the world. Such religious beliefs may or may not suite the climatic conditions of one's habitat.

So, in the 21st century, people should not be vegetarians or non-vegetarians by religion, they should choose to be herbivores or carnivores according to the climatic conditions.

Vegetarian and non-vegetarian food stuffs should be considered as elements of a meal without discrimination. Both consist of different nutrients and both types of food items should become a part of daily meals. Both play important roles in fulfilling the nutritive needs of the human body. The proportion should be decided on the basis of the nutritive value and their effects on the human body, depending upon the habitat and the availability of both vegetation and meat. The selection between vegetarian food and non-vegetarian food should not be influenced by religion. Instead, science should give direction to the choice. This uninfluenced choice of food would lead to completing the basic necessity of staple food – fulfilling the nutritive needs of the human body.

It has been believed that consumption of meats leads to aggression. This is true. However, it is also important to identify the reason behind this. Consumption of meat is accompanied with consumption of blood. This can be reduced by a tradition followed by the Muslims. This tradition is called Halal. It is a way in which the life of the prey is taken. Normally, the prey is killed in a single shot by cutting its neck. However, according to Halal, the prey is killed slowly. This has been misinterpreted as cruelty. There is a scientific reason behind this way of killing. If the prey's neck is cut, it dies due to lack of blood circulation in the brain. In other words, its brain dies, followed by the heart. In Halal, it is the other way around. The prey's body parts like legs, wings, etc. are cut, instead of cutting its neck. This way, the prey bleeds to death. Its heart dies first. This way, most of the blood is lost and the consumption of blood is minimised, almost none. This is an intelligent way of eliminating one of the biggest drawbacks of consuming non-vegetarian food.

The question here still remains; does blind faith still exist in the 21st century? Yes, it does. The reason behind this is lack of information caused due to misdirection and emphasis on the negatives instead of the positives. Most of the readers might find themselves thinking hard on why was it that they did not know this. The simple reason is misdirection. Halal is considered to be inhuman. It is considered to be cruelty. The scientific reason behind it has not been highlighted on a common forum that could reach the masses. This is the reason why the acceptance of this tradition is only limited to Muslims.

Now let's look at the cruelty towards animals. The most common example that each one of us can relate to is killing mice. Mice are killed by mouse traps, poison, etc. Nowadays, even the poison that is used is a slow poison as a precaution, so that it may cause minimum damage if consumed by humans. This works in the opposite way in case of mice. They have to tolerate a slow and painful death. Isn't this cruelty too? In this case, the cruelty is neglected and elimination of a disease spreading animal is emphasised.

Humans have a peculiar quality of moulding their observations in a way that would look positive or negative according to their choice or by the influence of religion, or the so called 'society' that they live in. This tendency leads to misdirection.

The conclusion of this chapter would be a simple change in the way we, the humans should think. Our choices should not be influenced. We should learn to look at both sides of the coin, instead of looking at the side that our religion or the society makes us look at. Science has all the answers. The study of the ways of life is very important.

It has the potential to change one's life and make it better, almost perfect.

CHAPTER THREE

A New Moon

A New Moon

New moon night is a night when the moon is not visible. A huge amount of negativity has been linked or perceived to have been originated from this night. For ages, this night has been considered to be unholy or evil.

In Hinduism, it is believed that one should not drive or travel on a new moon night. Many people have been following this blind faith for ages. Even in this so-called modern age, it is still being practiced. None of these people know the reason why it is unsafe to travel on such a night. They follow it blindly.

This blind faith came into existence in the time when electricity wasn't invented. Streets were dark due to the absence of streetlights. Moon light was the only source of light. It might seem strange that moon light was enough to lit up the streets. In the present time, streets are lit up with streetlights. We live in a concrete jungle. So, the lights in the buildings add up to the light.

Moon light hasn't lost its existence. The city lights are so bright that we fail to notice it. If we go to a village or someplace far away from the concrete jungle, we can notice the moon light .it may not be as powerful as the sun, but it is good enough to minimise the darkness of the night and make it favourable to travel.

On a new moon night, the absence of the moon is not noticed due to the city lights. But it was noticeable in the olden times. The vehicles of those times were bullock carts, horse carriages, etc. these were owned by the rich or the privileged. None of these had head lamps, tail lamps or any other kind of light. So, neither the road nor the other vehicles on it were visible. So, it wasn't safe to travel on a new moon night. These conditions made it almost impossible to avoid accidents. Also, there was a fair chance to be lost.

Darkness has dangers of its own. There is phenomenon that makes darkness unfavourable to travel. Our mind often plays games with us. Vision can be deceiving. Human eye can see objects when the light reflecting from them hits it. This light then creates a temporary image on the retina. This image stays on the retina for less than $1/10^{th}$ of a second. Then it is replaced by the next one. Sometimes, if it is not replaced by any other image, the previous one stays on the retina for a longer time. This happens because the image is still imprinted on the retina. So, the brain thinks that the object is still present and then it vanishes. This phenomenon is triggered by a sudden darkness or in other words, if the light is suddenly turned off. The absence of light means that no other image will be imprinted until light falls on the eye. Strange, isn't it? It is strange, but true. Try an exercise at home. Lock yourself in a dark room. Note: The room should be completely dark. Even a single ray of light can go against this phenomenon. Light up the room and concentrate on an object. Then turn off the light. You would be surprised to see the same object, even if there isn't a single ray of light. The object may not be clear. It might appear as a one-dimensional, flat, single coloured object. If you concentrate on a person, instead of an object in light, the same person may appear like ghosts that are shown in movies. Also, the image stays on the retina for less than second. After that, the retina is cleared. So, we think that the object vanished in thin air. It is practically impossible for an object to vanish in thin air. If we see a human figure instead of an object, we get scared. Our mind then reminds us of the stories that all of us have heard and/or seen in movies. So, our mind plays games with us, and we think that we've seen a ghost. This phenomenon must have been known to the people who initiated this blind faith.

The same thing happens on a new moon night. Even in today's time, there are places where not even a single source is available. One can often find such blind spots on a highway. Most of the highways do not have streetlights. This enhances vision, as the only source of light on such highways is the headlamps of vehicles. So, if the road is empty, then there is a fair chance that there won't be any source of light. Such blind spots are lit up by the moon light. But even this source of light is absent on a new moon night. So, it is believed that ghosts can be visible on a new moon night. The ghost that one sees or believes to have seen may or may not be real. They might merely be images imprinted on the retina.

There is one more phenomenon that adds up to the horror. Sound waves travel faster at night and also their range is increased. There is a scientific reason behind this. The temperature is low at night. Sound waves travel faster if the temperature is low. Silence adds up to both speed and range. If 2 or more sounds collide, each one of them loses speed and range. So, even sounds originating miles away can be heard. In olden times, nobody challenged blind faiths. So, everyone stayed at home on a new moon night. So, pin drop silence must have been a common thing on a new moon night. Even sounds that originated miles away could have been heard.

Whenever we hear a sound, we try to locate its origin. For example, if one hears someone else scream, then he/she tries to locate the person who is screaming. Imagine a situation when you can hear someone scream but fail to locate its origin. Wouldn't it sound strange? In such a situation, it is natural for anyone to think that it might have been a ghost that screamed.

The human mind has its own way to deal with mysterious inputs. It has an ability to find its origin. It starts playing games if it fails to find the origin or if some questions about it are left unanswered. For example, if we see something that looks like a human, but does not have a face, we conclude that it must be a ghost. Also, it vanishes in thin air. This confirms it to have been a ghost. The mysterious sounds, that originate miles away, add up to the horror. A perfect haunted atmosphere is created in our mind.

Now let's come back to the present times. Today, the streets are lit up with streets light and city lights. All the vehicles have headlamps, tail lamps, turn indicators, etc. so, we do not feel the need for the moon light. It is hardly noticeable. So, travelling on a new moon night is no longer dangerous. While travelling on such a night, one should make sure to check one's vehicle's lights. One should avoid travelling if the head lamps are dim or if the tail lamps aren't working. One should also expect to see or hear mysterious sounds. The understanding behind such mysterious inputs would automatically eliminate fear.

It's safe to travel on a new moon night. So, quit believing in this blind faith as it isn't applicable anymore. A new moon night is a symbol of a new beginning. The negativity linked with it should be eliminated.

A New Moon Night

A night when the moon is out of sight
We seldom call it a no moon night
We prefer to call it a new moon night
When the hope that is bright
But the absence of light
Makes the black (Blind faith), within us, out of sight
Even this night could be bright
But the black darkens our sight
We trap ourselves and stay out of sight
Seldom in our mind does it strike
That the light within us can make the night bright...

The Concept of God

The Concept of God

God was supposed to be a source of pure, white light, until some humans interrupted it with a prism and divided it into seven colours. These colours were then called religions. But we fail to understand all these colours originated from the same a single source of light. The creators of God did not intent to divide its followers into different religions; some impure souls introduced a prism and divided humans into different religions.

There are several religions. However, each one of them considers God as the most powerful entity. He is supposed to be the creator of the world and everything in it, including trees, animals and his greatest creation 'Human beings'. I perceive God in a completely opposite way. He is not the creator; human beings have created God.

God has different forms; Jesus for the Christians, Allah for the Muslims and Gods in 330 million forms for Hindus and a lot more. Every religion has is its own stories of his origin. He is supposed to be pure, an individual who does not have impurities like lust, greed, betrayal, etc. He is supposed to be the one who is perfect and unmatched.

Human beings cannot be compared with him. Naturally, this makes him powerful enough to destroy the world if its people do not follow the ways of life that have been laid and passed on across generations through his stories. This fear of mass destruction prevents us from going against any of his rules or through my perception, guidelines.

God came into existence or was brought into existence when the world was one place. There were no continents or countries. There weren't any governments to lay down laws or police to prevent the civilians from breaking them. The world was a free place. However, too much freedom led to total chaos. Animals could be controlled by the king of the jungle, lion; the simple reason behind this being that they only need to fulfil their basic needs – food and shelter. The design of the pyramid of life helped in maintaining a perfect balance. It is designed in such a way that it has the ability to fulfil the basic needs of all its elements. Vegetation is placed at the bottom as it has to cater both basic needs – food and shelter. It is then followed by the herbivores that thrive on it. Herbivores are followed by carnivores that survive by hunting the herbivores. Humans are supposed to be at the top, in the lowest possible quantity. However, fulfilling the basic needs was never enough for human beings. Unlike animals, human beings aren't satisfied even after fulfilling their basic needs. The greed to achieve more than the next person led to a search for new things. This then led to finding new ways of life all together. Some ways were harmless to others. However, some led a slow, but steady way towards destruction. Fear of death wasn't enough to create a discipline that would lead to peace and harmony. Means of communication were limited. Spreading a message or explaining the proper ways of life wasn't as easy as it is now. Nowadays, the ways of life can easily be explained through textbooks, internet, television, etc. Back then, the means of communication came with a lot of limitations. This led to the origin god. As mentioned in the 2nd paragraph, the followers did not have an option to question the ways of life laid by God. This was the time when man created God. God is an entity that cannot be seen or found.

In the beginning of the era of gods, the world was at peace. The simple reason behind this was leadership of God. A set of ways of life were laid. The ways of life were laid depending upon social status, profession, etc. The ways of life were set in a way that would suite one's lifestyle. Following them led to peace and also made sure that a balance was maintained in the society.

What is God? God is an illusion. He is an entity, which was created to control the world. He is the boogieman, the one that is used by parents to stop their children from being naughty, to stop them from going out of the way and follow their heart. He is supposed to control the world. However, we fail to understand that 'control' is an illusion.

God = Control

Control = Illusion

Hence, God = Illusion

Isn't that simple enough to understand?

God is worshipped in multiple forms. Some worship him in the form of an idol. They light candles in front of him, to keep him visible and glowing at all times, expecting him to light up their lives. They believe in him and expect him to deliver justice to their efforts. I fail to understand this. If God was so powerful, then why would he need candles to glow? If his followers believe in him, then why is his presence so important? Why is it so difficult and complicated to maintain his presence? I wonder why we need to need to follow a set of rituals to worship him. Rituals are often accompanied with festivals. Festivals are a mere excuse to come together and take a break from our busy, moneymaking lifestyles. Festivals have turned into holidays. Holidays are a pleasant memory to all. We plan them beforehand. They are so important that even banks are closed on those days. Every religion has its own way of celebrating these festivals. One thing remains the same – Unity. We fail to understand such a simple thing. Even the creators of God might not have expected anything else. Ask yourselves a question, that I often ask myself – What do these festivals mean to you? The only answer that you would find is – happiness, an excuse or even a liberty to follow your heart. Give gifts; make others happy, so that we can feel good about ourselves.

I am sure nobody must have noticed that previous paragraph contradicts my own statement - God is the boogieman, the one that is used by parents to stop their children from being naughty, to stop them from going out of the way and follow their heart. Children need to be trained to do the right thing. They are unaware of the consequence of their actions. I often compare life with a car. A car is driven by a trained driver. It has a steering wheel to turn it towards an appropriate direction. It has an accelerator to control its speed and a speedometer to monitor it too. It has brakes to stop it whenever needed to avoid any accidents. But I fail to understand, even after possessing all the necessary elements to maintain control, that promises a safe drive, yet accidents cannot be nullified. Several people still lose their lives, families shattered, lives put to an end. That's when we realise that control is an illusion. A new driver drives like a child. He bumps his car and causes a lot of trouble at times too. But experience is the best teacher. An experienced driver knows what to do in any situation, only after facing multiple situations. He knows what to do and what not to do. However, experience still fails to guarantee a bump free ride. That's another example that reminds us that control is an illusion. The only thing that a driver can do is go back in time and try to find the ways to drive safe. That's the only thing that he can do. Same goes with God. He is not meant to control its followers. He only tries to train them to drive. In the end, it is the driver who has to drive the car and try to reach the destination without getting hurt.

The intention behind writing this chapter is to send a message to all - keep driving, keep living your life. Look back into it and find out the mistakes and make sure that they aren't repeated. Don't treat God as a boogieman and follow his way, blindly. Don't be scared to be naughty at times. Go out of the way to follow your heart. If control wasn't an illusion, then why is that we need more than 330 millions of Gods to control us? Think of God as an entity that writes the rules but does not guarantee a smooth drive even after following them.

Don't think too much, life is short. Drive to the destination that your heart drives you to, because at the end of the day nothing in life can be controlled. So many traffic rules have been laid. Even law-abiding citizens, who follow all the rules, cannot guarantee a safe drive. A safe drive does not depend upon following or breaking the rules. The purpose of making rules is to restrict the possibilities of accidents by trying to control the traffic, so that all the drivers can experience a safe drive. Try to find out the purpose behind each and every rule. Drive fast, drive slow and even rash at times and try to stay in control, without a guarantee.

Use rules as guidelines and God as moral support. A better understanding of the purpose behind the rules would give you a reason to follow them. This reason would eliminate the need to memorise the rules; they would become a part of a richer and healthier lifestyle. This may not guarantee a safe drive, but a smoother drive for sure. It will give you a clearer picture. It will help you understand that the meaning of life isn't breathing, it means much more than that.

CHAPTER FIVE

Educate to Operate

Educate to Operate

Education, a word that is pretty simple to define, but a lot more complex to understand or perceive. Education is defined as: -

- (uncountable): the process or art of imparting knowledge, skill and judgment.

- (countable): facts, skills and ideas that have been learned, either formally or informally.

In today's world, the word 'education' is misunderstood. It is no longer an act of imparting knowledge; it is a means to get a degree or certificate. These certificates then become one's identity and are used to get jobs. Nobody is interested in imparting knowledge or learning new skills; all that the students want is a degree. Education is supposed to be an act that makes a student capable enough to work in an LOB (Line of business). Today's world is filled with a variety of LOBs like IT, engineering, accountancy, marketing, management, HR, etc.

Students can impart knowledge and skills by understanding and learning from the information stored in books. Teachers provide guidance to do so. It is their responsibility to help their students to learn from the books. Teachers are responsible to solve the queries of their students. However, it is the students' responsibility to present their queries and get them resolved from their teachers. The Indian education system is misinterpreted. It is interpreted or perceived to be a means to achieve a degree or certificate of expertise in a certain LOB. These degrees are achieved by clearing exams. These degrees are 80% theory based and 20% practical based. All that the students do is memorise each and every word from their books and notes and write them down on answer sheets. It is a question-and-answer system. There are a limited number of questions, and an answer is set for each one of them. So, the students do not need to understand the syllabus, they just need to memorise the answers to the limited set of questions. So, they develop a tendency to memorise the answers, instead of understanding the concept behind them. It has been observed that most of the students (even toppers) do not understand the concepts. This eliminates the curiosity in them. They do not try to understand or learn new concepts. Clearing the exams and achieving degrees isn't enough, the students need to score the maximum possible marks to survive the stiff competition. Education has become a race. The competition in this race is so stiff that even 1% marks can make a huge difference. The students are not left with any other option but to memorise all the answers word to word. It takes a long time to memorise the answers. So, they do not get the time to understand their meaning. But they fail to understand that a proper understanding of the concepts eliminates the need to memorise the answers. Unfortunately, even this option isn't open to them. The scoring system also works in the same way. The examiners are provided with a set of model answers. Even they do not check the answers; they just compare them with the model answers. The closest match gets the maximum marks. Students are treated like computers. They are programmed to answer a set of questions. The answers to each of the questions are stored in their memory. They just read the question and write down the answer, without even understanding the question. Even the 20% practical based exams work in the same way.

The definition of education has been changed. It isn't imparting knowledge; it has been changed to storing words in one's memory. Nobody looks at it as a means to impart knowledge or skills. The students do not learn or understand, all that they do is memorise the words that are printed in books and notes and write them down on the answer sheets.

This is another example of blind faith. The lack of curiosity leads to a blind faith in books, notes and other mediums that are meant to impart education. Even though the knowledge stored in these mediums is true, valid and has been proven to be so, the students or the recipients of this knowledge fail to make proper use of it. It is meant to gain expertise in a certain LOB. The lack of understanding leads to the elimination of the purpose of education. The purpose of education is to help an individual gather as much knowledge as possible, and to be able to apply it in his professional life. The lack of understanding goes against the purpose of education. The students fail to apply the knowledge as they do not understand it; all that they do is remember it in the form of words.

Not all students

Education is meant to qualify an individual to work in a specific LOB. However, many do not qualify to get jobs.

Unlike exams, the interviews do not have a set of question and answers. The interviewers ask questions that are applicable to the job profile that the candidate has applied for. They ask questions to check if the candidate is able to apply the knowledge required to work in that LOB. Since most of the candidates lack in application, they do not clear the interview. Instead of finding the reason of failure, they blame it on the competition. One of my friends, who is a CA (Charted Accountancy), narrated an incidence. A student of CA topped the exams in India. She was then offered jobs by the top ten companies in India. She applied for one of them. She was asked a couple of questions. She failed to answer those questions as she had scored the marks by memorising the answers; she lacked in application. She had also completed an article ship under the guidance of a CA. The purpose of this Article ship is to let the students work on field and get a proper understanding on how to apply the knowledge that they have gained. They receive the certificate of completion on the basis of their performance on field. The interviewers failed to understand why she lacked at application. When she was asked the reason behind this, she confessed that she had not worked on field. She had copied the worksheets that were prepared by other interns, who worked at the same firm. The interviewers not only rejected her, but also barred her from working as a CA for 3 years.

The purpose of education is to qualify to get a job. This candidate was the topper and so was that most eligible candidate that year. She not only failed to get a job, but also was forced to be jobless for 3 years.

This is a classic example of blind faith. It fits in the definition of blind faith, which is belief without true understanding, perception, or discrimination. It justifies that the students lack in application. This has become a severe problem these days. Many people fail to get a job even after achieving all the degrees that are required to qualify for a job. This problem is left unsolved. The key to solving a problem lies in the proper understanding of its cause. The cause of this problem is misinterpreted. The cause isn't competition; it is the lack of the ability to apply the knowledge.

The conclusion of this chapter lies in the right perception of looking at 'education'. It should be perceived as an act of imparting knowledge. There is no need to make any changes to the Indian education system. It is one of the most efficient systems in the world. Most of the leading companies, worldwide, may not be owned by Indians, but they are run by Indians. Several Indians are working as professionals in many such companies. The Indian education system should be interpreted as source of knowledge. There is a need of a proper understanding of this knowledge, instead of treating it yet another example of blind faith. This knowledge should not be memorised in the form of words, it should be understood, and one should learn to apply it. The proper application of this knowledge helps to qualify for working (operating) in the desired LOB. Instead of educating to memorise knowledge in the form of words, one should educate to operate.

Black or White

Black or White

'Black or white' or racism a plague that ruined any lives. Racism has been practised for 100's of years and even after several revolutions, it is still practiced. Many people are suffering, and some are fighting to stop it. Even today, in this new age world, people are discriminated on the basis of colour, religion, etc. However, we fail to understand the difference between discrimination and classification.

To understand the difference between discrimination and classification, it is important to study the Varna system.

Brahmins - Vedic priests

Kshatriyas – Kings, Rulers

Vaishyas – Cattle breeders, agriculturists, merchants, etc.

Shudras – Labourers, servants, etc.

The first 3 classes were together called the Arya or the Aryan race.

The Shudras were non-Aryans and were considered to be untouchable.

Varna system has its roots in Hinduism. Varna or colour was used to classify people. However, this wasn't the original idea behind the origin of this system. It was meant to classify people on the basis of their profession. The system got its name as people got their colour (skin colour) due to the environment that they worked in. The Brahmins were priests. They lived a pampered lifestyle. They weren't exposed to the sun. They lived in temples, ashramas and some even lived in huge mansions. The Kshatriyas were kings. So they lived a luxurious life too. They had all the comforts known to man. So, their skin never tanned. This naturally gave them a fair complexion and placed them at the top of the Varna system. The Vaishyas were bronze. Some of their professions were farming, pottery, etc. None of these professions gave them the liberty to live their lives like kings. They had to work in the sun and in harsh environments. Their lifestyles gave them a naturally tanned complexion. The Shudras or the Non-Aryans were labourers or servants. They were forced to work in harsh environments and weren't given any liberties. These conditions gave them a dark and unhealthy complexion. They were, hence, turned into untouchables. They did not have a social status, as they were at the bottom of the economy and hence, they were placed at the bottom of the Varna system.

This justifies how this system got its name – Varna (Colour).

The Varna system was formed with a sole purpose – classification, which was then misinterpreted as discrimination or racism. It also had a provision that gave its followers the liberty to change their profession. This provision was omitted by the Brahmins as it posed a threat to their superiority. Brahmins were priests and teachers. This gave them enough power to manipulate the system. They were paranoid and they also knew that if this freedom was given to all, then it would definitely pose a threat to their superiority and the change in lifestyle might have caused a change in skin colour (Varna). Instead of facing this threat, they decided to nullify its possibilities. This continued for centuries, until formal education was introduced. Education led to independence and also led to the end of the Kshatriyas (Kings). The world got divided into countries. People started to live in a civilised manner. This also led to formal education through schools, colleges, universities, etc. This brought light to the freedom to choose one's profession.

The Varna system might have faded but racism is still practiced. Even though Varna system has lost its existence, it is important to understand this system, so that its advantages can be used and its disadvantages, nullified.

Advantages of the Varna system: -

Classification: -

Classification is the first step to a healthy and prosperous civilisation. However, the classification should be on the basis of skills and the freedom to choose one's profession should be granted. It gives a better understanding of the responsibilities and the importance of the members of each element of classification. It also would lead to self-reliance as a nation, as all the necessaries and luxuries would be provided within the nation. This would minimise the need to import foreign goods.

Nurturing skills: -

Education begins at home. It is simpler to nurture skills if they are passed on through generations. The best example is 'family businesses. Family businesses have been a huge success. They grow bigger with every generation. This also applies to people who work on a salaried basis. There is a simple reason behind this theory.

Education begins at home. This means that our parents are the best teachers. They not only help us get the best education, but also support and help us all the way. Children are like clay. They can be moulded in any shape. Parents are responsible to give their children a proper shape. Hence, if they want their children to follow the same profession, then it becomes easier for them as they are the ones who mould them and nurture their skills. They can pass on the enterprise and also explain the details of the profession. Some details of any profession can only be understood through experience. It is impossible to understand any profession without practical experience. Every generation is exposed to a different work environment, depending upon the evolution of the market to adjust with constant change. This helps to develop skills right from the childhood. There are a lot of examples that justify the success of this theory. Most of the biggest names in all the businesses justify its success. Brand name like Reliance is one of the biggest names in India and has made it big in the international market as well. Brand names like these have been passed on through generations. Similar names are found in all the industrial sectors, right from the biggest brand names to the smallest industries like pottery, art, agriculture, etc. In fact, today's film industry has very few actors whose parents weren't in this industry. One can find enough examples to justify this theory.

It also justifies that the Varna system can take each profession to the next level from generation to generation. Each generation adds its contribution to the line of business. The next generation gets an opportunity to learn for the previous generations. This leads to the evolution of every profession and in turn leads to the evolution of the society a whole. It helps in making the world a better place.

Disadvantages of the misinterpreted Varna system: -
Racism or discrimination: -

The Varna system, if misinterpreted, leads to discrimination. Unlike classification, discrimination has a negative impact on the society. Discrimination leads to rage and rage leads to terrorism, which leads to the destruction of peace. It leads to unnecessary violence. The people who are strong in terms of social status are unaffected by this violence. However, the rest have to suffer the brutality of racism. This does not leave them with any other choice but to fight against it. The wise learn to ignore it, concentrate in improving their life and move on. However, the uneducated or the underprivileged spend their lives trying to fulfil their basic needs; the miserable life that they live leads to developing a negative attitude in them. Racism or discrimination acts as a fuel that makes the fire of negativity brighter and more hazardous. This fire burns all the opportunities of their development. Such people are then used by the political leaders. They offer them money, food, etc. in return of their votes. They lure such helpless people by promising them a fulfilling and prosperous life. Such promises are never fulfilled in the real sense. The puppets of the leaders do get a lot of wealth. They become wealthy, but not rich. The entire voting system is manipulated in this way. Apart from the leaders, no one else is profited.

Lack of freedom to choose one's profession: -

Availability of formal education has led to the end of this disadvantage. However, even today, the level of literacy is 74.04%. Even though this figure seems to be good, it needs a lot of work after looking at the current population. In 2011, the population of India was 124.1 Crores (1.241 billion). So, the number of illiterate people comes to 32.2

Crores (322 million). More than 32 Crore Indians are illiterate. The most important reason behind this is poverty. Poor people do not get an opportunity to get a formal education. Hence, they are forced either to follow the same profession as their parent or choose from limited professions. Their choice is limited to professions that are mainly consisting of physical labour. Such professions have very low wages. The wages are so low that they fail to fulfil even their basic needs. Due to this, it becomes impossible for them to get a formal education. They fail to provide it to their children. It becomes impossible for them to get out of this vicious circle. If we look at one of the previous chapters of this book – Educate to Operate, we will find that most of the people who get to opportunity to receive formal education do not have much of a choice to choose their profession. So, the freedom to choose one's professions seems to a mirage.

Stagnancy: -

The lack of freedom to choose one's profession leads to stagnancy. As mentioned in the chapter – *The Wealthy ain't Rich*; it is clear how this stagnancy works in the favour of the wealthy. It only not helps them maintain their positions at the top, but also restricts the rest from reaching their level.

Education is meant to give an individual a sense to lead a rich life. It is also meant to provide an opportunity to nurture one's skills, make use of the freedom choose one's profession. In short, it is meant to promote the advantages of the Varna System and eliminate the disadvantages of its misinterpretation. Education and the Varna system have many things in common. Both can be a blessing if interpreted in the right way and a curse if misinterpreted. Both can be misused to discriminate. The Varna system was misused to discriminate on the basis of religion and education is misused to discriminate on the basis of social status. The British introduced a phenomenon- provide the poor with food, shelter and education and they will be your slaves. Before independence, the poor were offered a house, food, money and a formal education for the price of converting themselves into Christians. This was then used against them. God has always been considered as the Almighty, the one who shows us the right or the appropriate path to follow. He creates rules that cannot be questioned or broken. Likewise, even today, religion has become the key to divide. Every religion has its own set of rules. All these sets of rules define the lifestyle of the followers of these religions. The set of rules of each religion is different from each other, which in turn create a difference in lifestyle. This difference in lifestyle helps in dividing people into groups and forces them to fight against each other. None of the Gods ask its followers to fight against each other. This is a classic example of misinterpretation. Since the rules put forward by each religion cannot be questioned, it becomes easier to manipulate them, so that they can be used to drive the followers of different religions to fight against each other.

The British found out that it was easier to rule using a weapon - divide and rule. India gained freedom from them but failed to gain freedom from the weapon that was used by them. We are still fighting amongst each other. Even though it is simple enough to understand, the weapon is still being used. The only difference is that before independence, the trigger was pulled by the British, now it is being pulled by the politicians.

The result is still the same, the common man is shot. The only reason behind all this is our busy lifestyles. People are so busy earning money that they do not have any other reason, but to ignore and tolerate it; learn to live with it. Tolerating injustice is even worse than committing it.

Even after more than 60 years of independence, India is a developing nation. We have learned to blame our political leaders for this. The real reason behind this is the weapon – divide and rule. So, instead of discriminating, a better understanding of the means to classify is the only way to stop this weapon from firing.

CHAPTER SEVEN

Television = Hypnotism

Television = Hypnotism

Television is a media that is accessed by the masses. It is present in every home and is watched on daily basis. It was once called and idiot box, as it does not benefit its users in any manner. It only makes them lazy (couch potatoes) and wastes their time. The most popular shows on TV, these days, are daily soaps. Watching daily soaps is not a habit, it has become an addiction. The viewers (victims of this addiction) don't fail to watch their favourite shows. They even plan their daily chores, so that they would get time to watch such shows. They fail to identify this as an addiction; they prefer to call it a habit. They are not at fault. These shows are meant to be addictive, so that they can be used to induce hypnosis.

Hypnotism is a great stage show. In such a show, the hypnotiser induces hypnosis in volunteers, chosen amongst the audience. There are several methods of inducing it. The most important aspect in these methods is fixation. Fixation is defined as: -

Fixation (psychology) - The state in which an individual becomes obsessed with an attachment to another human, an animal, or an inanimate object

Fixation (visual) - Maintaining the gaze in a constant direction

As defined, fixation (visual) means maintaining the gaze in a constant direction. The hypnotiser asks his subject to concentrate on a specific object. The fixation isn't limited to vision. He then starts narrating some events slowly, slower than how a narrator would narrate the same event. These stories slow down the subject's thinking process and eventually the subject closes his eyes. This induces a special state of mind called hypnosis. Hypnosis has been defined as "a special psychological state with certain physiological attributes, resembling sleep only superficially and marked by a functioning of the individual at a level of awareness other than the ordinary conscious state." This definition captures our common understanding of hypnosis, but research has not only revealed that hypnosis is a much more complicated thing, but it has also given rise to a number of theories about how to best define hypnosis. One theory suggests that hypnosis is a mental state, while another theory links hypnosis to imaginative role-enactment. Persons under hypnosis are said to have heightened focus and concentration with the ability to concentrate intensely on a specific thought or memory, while blocking out sources of distraction. Hypnosis is usually induced by a procedure known as a hypnotic induction involving a series of preliminary instructions and suggestions. The hypnotic suggestions may be delivered by a hypnotist in the presence of the subject or may be self-administered ("self-suggestion" or "autosuggestion"). The use of hypnotism for therapeutic purposes is referred to as "hypnotherapy", while its use as a form of entertainment for an audience is known as "stage hypnosis".

(Courtesy of Wikipedia: http://en.wikipedia.org/wiki/ Hypnosis#Induction)

Once the volunteer is hypnotised, he develops a blind faith in the hypnotizer. This gives the hypnotizer an opportunity to make his volunteer believe whatever he tells him and act accordingly. It is an amusing show to watch.

The daily soaps are similar to hypnotism. They bear an abstract resemblance. This resemblance is not noticed. It is yet another method of self-suggestion. The intentions of inducing hypnosis are achieved. Such shows get registered in the viewers' memory, permanently. The viewers remember each and every detail. These soaps are directed in a way that enhances fixation. Slow motion, slow zoom-in are some of the techniques used. The reactions of each character are captured. This helps in slowing down the flow and also enhances concentration. The eyes and mind of the viewers are glued to the TV screen. The pace of the story is slow. Nothing much happens in an episode. Even if the viewers watch one episode per week, they will not miss anything. The slow speed helps in fixation, which in turn converts the habit into an addiction. The finishing scene of each episode is left incomplete in order to compel the viewers to watch the next episode. The bond of an incomplete end is the strongest bond. It can be compared with an incomplete task or a breach in thought process. An incomplete task is like an unfinished product or an uncut diamond; it is useless till the time it is completed. This does not leave the viewers with any other choice, but to wait anxiously for almost 24 hours to watch the next episode. The stories of such soaps sink so deep in the viewers' minds, that they cannot live without watching them on a daily basis. This also compels them to discuss the story with their friends and family.

All this is done to increase the TRP (Target Rating Point) of daily soaps. This TRP is used to decide the charge per second for the advertisements that are shown in the breaks. A higher TRP leads to a higher revenue generation. This revenue is shared between the producers of the channel and the daily soaps. It is pretty simple for them. They do not need to work hard on writing the stories; all that they need to do is slow down the pace. A huge amount of revenue is generated.

All this explains the similarity between TV and hypnotism, fixation and suggestion being the most important similarities between the two. The only difference is that the viewers of soaps aren't hypnotised, completely. They are induced in a trance that helps them access their subconscious mind. This helps in increasing the sales of the products that are advertised in the breaks. As mentioned earlier, the subject (once hypnotised) develops a blind faith in the hypnotizer. In the same way, the viewers develop a blind faith in the products or the brands that are advertised in the breaks. The viewers are unaware of this. So, whenever they go to the market to buy a product, they recall specific brands. These brands are the brands that are advertised in the breaks of their favourite shows. Most of the brands offer similar features; the difference in price isn't high either. The brands only need to concentrate on advertising their products on TV. They need to select daily soaps on the basis of their TRP.

This is a classic example of misdirection. The brands can penetrate through the viewers' minds and register their products in the viewers' subconscious minds. This helps in their sales, as the viewers develop a blind faith and don't think much before buying a product, they do not think about their requirements either. They also buy products that they don't even need.

TV is often referred to as an idiot box. Now it should be referred to as a medium of inducing hypnosis. Nobody has brought light to this similarity, only because it won't work if highlighted. This is a well-designed technique, used by the wise to make a lot of money. The viewers or the victims are unaware of this.

Stopping people from watching daily soaps isn't the idea behind writing this chapter; the idea is to generate awareness about the addiction. TV is a great source of entertainment. It should be watched wisely, keeping in mind that it might turn into an addiction. The viewers should watch selected soaps, instead of watching as many as possible. It has been observed that housewives watch as many daily soaps as possible in their free time, as they do not have any other medium of entertainment. There are a lot of other ways of entertainment. Hobbies like reading books, listening to music are the best and the most convenient examples. The addiction to TV has led to ignorance to the hobbies. The worst impact is that it eats up the time that could be used to spend some quality time with family. Nowadays, everyone is busy. Most of the time is spent in earning money or the prepare oneself to do so (education). The members of a family get very less time to spend with each other. Most of it is wasted because of this addiction. This creates an emotional disconnect between the members of the family. This affects the emotional attachment as well. The lack of emotional attachment becomes a reason for a lot of family problems. The members of a family only live together till the time they become independent. The children don't get time to share their problems with their parents. They do not clarify their curiosities (about adulthood) with their parents. They try to find their answer through TV, internet, etc. Most of the soaps are based on families that are bound together with money or family heritage. Jealousy, rage, harassment and many other negative emotions are highlighted. The viewers compare their lives with the ones shown on TV. They even develop such negative emotions within themselves. They judge others based on the characters shown in daily soaps. They also develop many misconceptions. They develop a blind faith in the soaps. This blind faith also adds up to the lack of emotional attachment. This impacts the moral values that the children develop. The families that are shown in the daily soaps do not possess high moral values; most do not have any either. The only things that are highlighted are money and family heritage. The viewers, unknowingly, develop a similar attitude. Fixation not only registers the brands, but also registers such negative emotions in the subconscious minds of the viewers.

Children leave their parents once they start earning money. Money is the most important thing that binds many families. This might sound harsh, but it is true. Retired parents become a liability and are forced to live alone or to live in old age homes. People fail to understand the value of the guidance that their (elderly and experienced) parents provide.

The popularity of TV has reached its peak. It is impossible to find a home without TV. TV wasn't this popular till the late 90's of the last century. The popularity of TV has increased, drastically and so has the rate of divorce and helpless senior citizens.

It is important to understand the consequence of the addiction of watching TV. Before developing an addiction to TV, there was a time when families spent more time together. They spent quality time with each other. They did not need reason like festivals, family functions, marriage ceremonies, etc. to meet their relatives. Life was much more fulfilling back then; money wasn't as important either. Money was earned to satisfy the needs and luxuries of their families. Nowadays, earning money is no longer a need; it has become a compulsion to win the race of social status. The feeling of living with a family has lost its beauty; it has become a mere compulsion to live with one's parents, till one becomes financial independent. Divorce has become a common thing these days and so are helpless parents. Parents become nothing but a liability once they retire and stop earning money. The introduction of soap operas in TV is a landmark that defines the difference between a family and a group of people that are financially co-dependent on each other.

TV is a great source of entertainment. Watching TV isn't a bad habit, till it becomes an addiction. It is a weapon, used by the wise, to create social distress that helps to create a society that is unstable. This also helps them overcome the fear of losing their position at the top, as such social and emotional development restricts the possibility of self-development. A wiser and a more serious outlook towards TV is today's requirement.

The following poem is an attempt to take a glance at the feelings of retired parents who have been abandoned...

You are a part of me...

You are a part of me...

I can feel you inside of me

Feeding on me, till you can be

Now you have stepped outside of me

But you are dependent on me

You feed on me, till need be

Now you ain't feeding on me

But all that you get is from me
I hold your hand, show you the way
You take your first step holding my hand
Till you fly up, up and away
Now you no longer need me
So, you send me away
But all I need you to know
Wherever you want me to be
You will always be a part of me...

Too much Prayer makes one a Prey

Too much Prayer makes one a Prey

Prayer has always been considered to be a way to communicate with God. God, the Almighty, has a solution to all the problems, also has the ability to grant wishes, make life better and smoother. A daily dose of prayer is considered to be the best way to keep one away from trouble and guarantee a smoother life. Prayer is a day starter for its followers. It is the first thing that they do. In today's busy lifestyle, people do not have time for anything else, but work (moneymaking). So, they pray so fast that it sounds like murmuring. They remember the prayers word-to-word, without any clue about their meaning; it is same as the misinterpretation of education.

Nobody has the time or inclination to find out the importance of prayers. It is a height of blind faith. Prayers are a poetic collection of the ways of living a rich and fruitful lifestyle. If the prayers are read and understood, one would find them to be the same as the concept of God.

The ignorance towards finding out the meaning behind prayers isn't the only reason why their meaning isn't known to all, there is one more reason. The prayers are written in a language that is not known to a common man. The priests are religious scholars. They know all the languages that are known to man or at least the languages used in their religion. In Hinduism, the prayers were written in Sanskrit. Sanskrit was a language that wasn't known to anyone other than the Brahmins. So, they were the only ones who could understand the meaning behind the prayers.

Hiding the real meaning behind the prayers wasn't the intension behind this. Prayers are written in a language that is not only difficult to comprehend, but also using words that are difficult to pronounce. It takes a lot of concentration and dedication to remember and say such prayers. The level concentration required to remember and pronounce the prayers is so high that it turns into fixation. This fixation makes one forget about everything else. In such a state of mind, the mind is cleared and the only thing on one's mind is the prayers. The words sound as if they were the only sounds that existed. The subconscious mind is accessible, and the prayers get registered in it. However, the lack of comprehension of the meaning of these prayers eliminates the purpose of registration. As mentioned earlier, the prayers were written in a language that wasn't comprehensible to the common man. So, if not comprehended, the prayers get registered as a set of words that do not make any sense. This questions the purpose of prayers. Prayers are nothing but a means to induce hypnosis. This makes the priest a hypnotiser and makes him a superhuman. His superpower is ability to induce hypnosis. Since the prayers are not comprehended, the priest explains their meaning. The prayers induce a state of hypnosis which leads to the registration of a certain values in the followers' minds, permanently, as they get registered in their subconscious minds. The registration of these values leads to the formation of behavioural trends.

The access to the subconscious mind is divine. This access is yet another example of suggestion. Hypnosis is a special state of mind in which the registration of prayers is not the only purpose; the purpose is much higher. The real purpose behind all this is to condition the mind by setting up certain ways of life; good and bad are defined. A certain set of values get registered in the subconscious minds of the followers, religion wise. A standardisation is achieved, that eliminates most of possibilities of a difference in opinion. This technique was useful in the olden times as it brought peace in the society. This led to a healthy and prosperous society. A society is nothing but a group of people living together. In the olden times, this society consisted of people belonging to the same religion. So, their values were the same. This is a unique form of value education. This process is called 'inception'.

Inception is defined as the creation or beginning of something; the establishment.

This standardisation of values can be compared with communication. Two or more people communicate and understand each other if they speak in the same language. In the same way, if all the members of a society possess the same values, they understand each other and live in peace. Values help in differentiating between right and wrong, good and bad, ethical and unethical and so on. A person's identity or his personality is defined by his sense to differentiate between right and wrong. He takes decisions and lives his life on the basis of this sense of differentiation.

So, if a person possesses a proper sense of differentiation, he becomes capable enough to take the right decisions, becomes successful and lives a rich and prosperous life. The process of registering values acts as a light that shows the right path of life. Each religion has its own God, and each God has its own values. So, a difference in opinion is observed in people following different religions.

It is rightly said that God has answers to every question. Whenever a person is in dilemma, or is not able to take the right decision, he prays. This sends him back to the state of hypnosis and helps him recall the values that have been inculcated in his mind. This helps him to differentiate between right and wrong. He is then able to take the right decision.

A person who devoted his life to religious purposes is supposed to have a pure soul. Pure is defined as a substance that is not mixed or adulterated with any other substance or material. The word 'pure' correctly defined the soul of such an individual. He spends of his time praying and listening to the lectures (pravachana). In short, such individuals are repeatedly induced in the state of hypnosis. They consider the priests to be some kind of an avatar of God. This eliminates the possibilities of inculcating any values, other than the values that are inculcated by their priests. So, their souls are pure as they aren't adulterated by any other values. They develop a blind faith in such priests.

As explained in the earlier chapter, 'The Concept of God', God is considered to be the Almighty, the most powerful entity, the one who cannot be challenged. This makes such pure souls defenceless, as they are controlled by priests, an avatar of God.

The two words, 'pray' and 'prey', are words with similar spellings. The only difference is the third letter. There is a striking similarity in their definitions too.

Pray is defined as: -

- To petition or solicit help from a supernatural or higher being.

- To humbly beg a person for aid or their time.

- To communicate with God for any reason.

Prey is defined as: -

Noun

1. An animal hunted or caught for food; quarry.

2. One that is defenceless, especially in the face of attack; a victim.

3. The act or practice of preying.

Verb

1. To hunt, catch, or eat as prey: Owls prey on mice.

2. To victimize or make a profit at someone else's expense.

3. To plunder or pillage.

4. To exert a baneful or injurious effect

As mentioned earlier, the pure souls are defenceless and as defined, a prey is defenceless too. The similarity in the two words, 'pray' and prey', lies in being defenceless. If a priest decides to become a hunter, then he can easily turn his followers into his prey. He can control them like puppets and make profit on their expense by making demands on the name of donation. So, the difference between praying and to be preyed lies in the intentions of the priest. This justifies the title: -

'Too much prayer makes one a prey'

History justifies the title too. In Medieval England, the Medieval Church was more powerful than what it is today. Everybody's life was dominated by the Church. All the people - village peasants or people living in towns - believed that God, Heaven and Hell all existed. Right from childhood, the people were taught that the only way they could get to Heaven was if the Roman Catholic Church let them. Everybody was terrified of Hell and the people were told that about the horrors of Hell in the weekly services they attended. Church had total control over the people. Peasants worked for free on Church land. This proved difficult for peasants as the time they spent working on Church land, could have been better spent working on their own plots of land producing food for their families. They paid 10% of what they earned in a year to the Church (this tax was called tithes). Tithes could be paid in either money or in goods produced by the peasant farmers. As peasants had little money, they almost always had to pay in seeds, harvested grain, animals etc. This usually caused a peasant a lot of hardship as seeds, for example, would be needed to feed a family the following year. What the Church got in tithes was kept in huge tithe barns; a lot of the stored grain would have been eaten by rats or poisoned by their urine. A failure to pay tithes, so the peasants were told by the Church, would lead to their souls going to Hell after they had died. This is one reason why the Church was so wealthy. The Church also did not have to pay taxes. This saved them a vast sum of money and made it far wealthier than any king of England at this time.

Another example of the misuse of this phenomenon is terrorism. Some priests decide to become hunters. They misuse the access to the followers' subconscious minds. They manipulate the religious values. Instead of inculcating values that ensure peace, they inculcate values that make their followers violent. The followers develop hatred towards the followers of other religions. Such followers are then led on the path of terrorism. The priests claim that this path would lead to heaven.

The difference between praying and to be preyed lies in the intentions of the priest. It is almost impossible to find out the intentions of the priest. Hence, it is important to find out the meaning of the prayers by learning the language that the prayers are written in, instead of believing the priest, blindly. A knife is used by both doctors and murderers. A doctor uses it to save lives and a murderer uses it to take lives. The results of their actions are opposite. The difference in the results lies in the difference in their intentions.

Act of praying can be used as a means of self-suggestion (inducing a state of hypnosis without anyone else's assistance or guidance). It provides access to the subconscious mind. The subconscious mind is much more powerful than the conscious mind. The access to the subconscious mind is beneficial in several was. It is much more stable than the conscious mind. It provides the strength to take a broader outlook towards life and makes it easier to take the right decision; starting the day by praying helps in making it fruitful. It is useful to students, as the access to the subconscious minds lets them store knowledge in their memory, permanently.

This chapter may be misinterpreted to be anti-religious, although it is not intended to. It is intended to signify that the act of praying can be beneficial or hazardous, depending upon the priest's intentions. The key to making it beneficial, lies in the proper understanding of the prayers and the values that are intended to be inculcated by the followers of any religion. The religious values of all the religions are rich and have the intended to ensure peace and harmony in the society by inculcating proper values in its followers' minds.

CHAPTER NINE

Puppets of the Wise

Puppets of the Wise

In India, a battle has been fought for ages. A battle is fought between two or more sides with opposite opinions or opinions that are different from each other. These opinions come from the variety of perspectives that each one of us has, to look at things or in this case our cultural values. This does not change the values that have been laid and passed on from generation to generation.

The difference in perspective exists due to various reasons like financial status, education, society, etc. For example, if a half-filled glass of water is kept in front of a poor or underprivileged person; he would drink it and also keep some for his family. If the same glass is kept in front of a wealthy businessman, he would start thinking of ways to sell it. The reason behind the difference in perspective in this case is 'difference in financial statuses'. A poor person is incapable of fulfilling his basic needs. On the other hand, wealthy businessman is not only capable of fulfilling his basic needs but exceed them and live a luxurious life. So, the value of the half-filled glass of water is different to them. This causes the difference in their perspectives.

Similarly, in the new age world, we have the freedom to decide or choose between the cultural values like being vegetarian or non-vegetarian, to be a follower of God or not to be, etc. We try to follow the rules that suit our lifestyles. Nobody has the time or inclination to find out the reason behind these rules. We classify them into faith and blind faith. We try to avoid blind faith and in the 21st century, the educated and the civilised or the so-called modern individuals have eliminated blind faith from their lifestyles. However, if we go through the earlier chapters, we will find that blind faith hasn't lost its existence. The only thing that has changed is the form of faith or the rules that we follow, blindly. The proper understanding of blind faith led to this conclusion. Hence, it is important to understand the meaning and the purpose of the rules or the cultural values, which were laid down thousands of years ago.

India is considered to be rich in culture. It is also considered to be the oldest and richest civilisation.

Lord Macaulay addressed to the British Parliament on 2nd February 1835: -

"I have travelled across the length and the breadth of India, and I have not seen one person who is a beggar, who is a thief. Such wealth I have seen in this country, such high moral values, people of such high calibre, that I do not think we would ever conquer this country, unless we break the very backbone of the nation, which is her spiritual and cultural heritage and therefore, I propose that we replace her old and ancient education system, her culture, for if Indians think that all that is foreign and English is good and greater than their own, they will lose their self-esteem, their native culture and they will become what we want them to be, a truly dominated nation."

This paragraph described the real India, a rich prosperous and wealthy nation with high cultural values. However, the latter half describes the means to weaken the same nation and turn it into a poor, underdeveloped nation. Lord Macaulay must have been an astrologer. He predicted the current condition of India almost 200 years back. The means were simple- replace her old and ancient education system, her culture, for if Indians think that all that is foreign and English is good and greater than their own, they will lose their self-esteem, their native culture and they will become what we want them to be, a truly dominated nation.

This is truly what India is like these days. We have lost our self-esteem; our native culture and we also think of foreign goods to be better than our own. Please try an exercise- look at your car or bike, your mobile phone and all your belongings. I am sure, most of them would be foreign or made by foreign companies. Even after more than 60 years of independence, it is unchanged. Even the language used for commercial purposes is English, instead of our national language- Hindi. Hindi, our national language is only used for entertainment (movies, daily soaps, music, etc.). The reason behind this is that is a language that most of us can understand. So, it has a potential to make these means of entertainment popular and the producers can make a lot of money out of it. This is such a shame. None of the foreign countries do so. This is a mere example of how we have lost our own education system and cultural values. Our education system is an integral part of our cultural values. It isn't anything different than that. If we look at our cultural values, they can teach us anything and everything that we need to live a rich and prosperous life. The Varna system is a classic example. It teaches us to classify people on the basis of their profession. These professions are nothing but a division of responsibility to provide the basic necessaries in life and also the luxuries. However, even such a rich system has been misinterpreted and slowly, but steadily eliminated from our lives. Ignoring such rich cultural values have turned things around. As mentioned in Lord Macaulay's speech, India was a rich and prosperous nation. It did not have a single beggar or thief. This condition has been reversed. Now India is a nation full of beggars and thieves. A large chunk of the population is below the level of poverty. The level of corruption is also very high. And last but not the least, it is a dominated nation; a nation that is developing and is being dominated by all the developed nations. Try to imagine India without any foreign goods, it would sadly, but surely be a nation without any luxuries. Even the basic needs would not be fulfilled. It would be nothing, but a landmass inhabited by uneducated, hungry and uncivilised beggars and thieves. I am sure, there won't be even a single theory that has not only been successful to turn things around in the opposite direction, but also the condition is still unchanged.

This may seem to be harsh, but, sadly, it is the true picture of our nation. This is the very reason to understand our cultural values and try to make them a part of our lifestyles. A battle was triggered by the British and is still being fought within our minds, the minds of Indians. This battle is being fought between Indian and foreign cultures. We still find foreign goods and culture to be richer than our own. However, we fail to understand that we have lost all the wealth and prosperity due to this fight. Another battle is also being fought within the nation. This battle has more than two sides. It is fought on the basis of religion, caste and even on the basis of place of birth (state).

India is a gun loaded with bullets. It has the calibre to be rich and self-reliant. However, the trigger is foreign. So, even after being a gun loaded with bullets of calibre and skills, it is useless because it is trigged by foreign culture instead of its own.

Lord Macaulay's speech was circulated online through emails and posts on social networking websites. It turned into a conspiracy. This speech has been proved to be a fraud and it has also been justified that it was not written by Lord Macaulay. Let's not get into the details, as they are available online. It is not important whether the speech is genuine or a fraud. This speech may not be true, but it describes India as it was before being invaded by the British. It may be an exaggerated version of the true condition of India. It is true that it wasn't possible not to find even a single beggar or thief. It is also true that the moral values weren't that rich either. India was filled with blind faith, racism or casteism. Unity was never seen in India. It was ruled by foreigners like Mughals, Portuguese, etc. However, the British successfully ruled the entire nation, singlehanded.

This speech is a perception. It may or may not be true, as perceptions are not meant to be true or false. It is a perception, not a rule or some kind of a definition. Being a perception, it is a waste of time to check if it is genuine or not. We Indians have always been ruled, we have never been rulers. This speech talks about a way to make it simpler for the foreigners (British) to rule India. Isn't it simple enough to understand that it tells that India was ruled by using a simple way- divide and rule? India was divided even before the British knew about it. So, it became even simpler for them. Nothing has changed. Even today, India is divided. It was united for some time to gain freedom from the British. Sadly, this unity didn't last long, or it wasn't meant to last longer than that.

All this also suggests one more thing; we Indians are people who can easily be ruled, not only because of the lack of unity, but also because of our perception. This takes us back at the beginning of this chapter. A poor or a needy person would look at it as a consumable item. In this case, that person isn't consuming it, as it is proved to be a fraud. He is busy trying to check its purity. However, a wealthy businessman would look at it as a weapon to rule. Hence, it isn't important to check if this speech is genuine or not. It should be looked at like a comparison between what India is and what it could have been. It is a classic example of the means to rule a rich country like India.

All this justifies that that it is easy to rule India, as we Indians are puppets; puppets that are tied using invincible strings. This is a classic example of invincibility. Even though each one of us is tied with them, we fail to notice. Life has become very expensive. So, earning money is a must, no matter what it takes. In India, every person who earns money spends 12 hours or even more at work. We no longer earn to live; we live to earn. So, we do not have time for ourselves. The free time that we scrape out of our busy lifestyles is spent sitting in front of an idiot box – Television. These strings are strong enough to control us because of one reason – self-proclaimed elimination of blind faith. Instead of learning a lesson from this speech, it has been proven to be useless or even worse, a fraud.

If we compare ourselves (Indians) with puppets, we will find that the puppets haven't gained freedom not because the strings are strong or difficult to break; the puppets are still controlled by puppeteers because of the self-proclaimed elimination of blind faith.

This should be good enough to justify the title of this chapter –

Puppets of the wise.

CHAPTER TEN

A Petition for the Cause

A Petition for the Cause

After celebrating Hope's 10th birthday, her parents find peace of mind in their bedroom. After tucking in their overjoyed daughter, they sit on their bed and recall the party. The proud husband pats his wife's back, praising her for the efforts in organising such a great party. Wife thanks him for coming back home early, so that he could attend his daughter's birthday party and reminds him that all this would've been incomplete without his presence. After gliding into the clouds of happiness and celebration, they put their feet on the ground and come back to reality. Suddenly, they notice a letter written to them by their daughter. The mother picks it up, expecting a token of appreciation from her daughter. She starts reading it and bursts into tears. She hands the letter over to her husband but fails to find words to describe the reason for crying. The letter starts: -

Dear Mom and Dad,

Thanks for the wonderful party that you arranged. Thanks to dad for coming home early; I don't recall meeting him before sleeping, since we have moved to this big house. I only get to see a glimpse of him before going to school. Today he spent a lot of time with me; I wish my birthday could come once every week, instead of once every year. I was also glad to see so many people in the house; otherwise, I wonder why we need such a big house, when we hardly spend any time in it. All of us wake up in the morning to go to the same places each day. You guys go to work, and I go to school. I always watch mom running behind me and dad, to help us get ready. Then the maid serves us the breakfast and we all dress up to go to the places, where we spend most of our time. I go to school and both of you have to go to work.

The other day, our English teacher read out a story of a man who sells toys and balloons outside a park. He works all day to earn money. He lives in a small house in a slum. When I asked my teacher how small it was, she told me that it was even smaller than my bedroom that she had seen at our housewarming party. He has two children - a son and a daughter. They go to school together. They all eat breakfast together. Then he goes to the park on his bicycle and his children walk to the school together. On their way to school, Munni and Sonu pluck fruits from the trees by the road. After coming back home, they find their mom waiting for them. They don't need to go to the boring day care centre that I have to go to everyday. They drink a glass of milk and go to play with their friends who live in the same slum. I wonder where I would play. Our society does not have a ground to play on and I hardly know any of our neighbours' kids. Then she kept talking about the games that they played. I don't remember their names, as I never even heard about them till then. I was shocked, as I play games only on my tablet. After some time, when it gets dark, they go back home to meet their father, who comes back home at the same time. They run to him as he gets toffees for them every day. He then asks them to talk about what they learned in school that day. He thanks them for teaching him new things. Teacher said that he had never gone to school in his life. I thought that these guys must be aliens from a different planet because whenever I ask you guys about why I have to go to school you tell me that everyone needs to go to school so that when I grow old, I would get a job in a good company and earn money to raise a family. The family then eats dinner together and then they all go to sleep.

I thought Sonu and Munni are so lucky. They don't have to wait for their birthday to spend time with their mom and dad. Their mom does not work, and their dad comes back the same time they come back after playing games that have never even heard of. They don't have a big house like ours'. I always wonder why we need so many rooms, when we can sleep in one. We hardly spend any time at home. All we do at home is eat and sleep. We never get to spend time together. Let us shift in a smaller house, so that mom won't need to work. I have always heard you guys talking that it would be impossible to pay for the big house if she does not work. Dad, why don't you start selling toys outside the park that we go to every weekend? You can start by selling the toys that I got today. You can even take my bicycle. I never asked for a big house. I don't need a separate room for myself. I loved sleeping in your room in our old house. Please tell me if this is possible, because none of my friends live a life like this.

This letter is a petition for the cause of changing the meaning of the word 'Family'. It's the same story in each house. The question that the ten-year-old asked at the end of the letter is simple. All she wanted to know was whether it was possible to live a life with her family in a small house, rather than living a big house, that is empty all day.

Each chapter of this book talks about the conflict between dictionary meaning of words and the ways that they could be perceived. A theist memorises and follows the dictionary meanings, without event understanding the real meaning behind them. On the other hand, an atheist reads the meaning and doesn't even bother to memorise it, as he is smart enough to know that the words in a dictionary are arranged alphabetically, so that they would be easily accessible, when needed. He makes up his own perception; a perception that is purely his own. He is not blinded by religion, God or ways of life, set by the so called rich and successful personalities. He does not fear what others would think, as he knows that the race to fulfil the ever-growing wants won't let him focus on his needs. He knows the true meaning to life is to live it. Unlike an atheist, a theist only survives in the ever-growing competition. Success lies in living a life on your own terms, not in blindly tracing others'.